THE TRAVAILS OF KING AKALOR

HALIMA ONOJA

The Travails of King Akalor
All Rights Reserved.
Copyright 2023 by Halima Onoja
No part of this publication may be reproduced, distributed, or transmitted in any form or by any means, including photocopying, recording, or other electronic or mechanical methods, without the prior written permission of the author, except as permitted by U.S. copyright law. Permission requests go to halimaonoja@gmail.com / abenema2000@yahoo.com
+23407038067773/08065169673

For privacy reasons, some names, locations, and dates may have been changed.

Book Cover by Nokot Boryo
Illustrations by Abraham A

ISBN: 978-1-7363-889-7-6 (Print)
ISBN: 978-1-7363889-6-9 (Ebook)

PRINTED IN THE UNITED STATES OF AMERICA

OLABOOKS INTERNATIONAL
MY BOOK • MY PASSION

http://www.olabooksinternationalselfpub.com

Dedication

In Affectionate Greeting to
A Royal Father of Nations, A Servant, A Bridge Builder Per Excellence and A Peace Maker, King James O. Akalor. Who lately joined the Ancestors.

And for living lives that lit this piece. This is for
Joan A. Abraham (PJ), Arian A. Abraham (PA) & … … The No Ordinary Children.

For sustaining life and inspiring my everyday deep imagination and creativity, this is also for a living legend, an angel incarnate, and a perfect humanist, **Abraham E.A.**

And for all those who somehow found space in their hearts to create a home for me.

Contents

Act One **1**
   Scene One 1
   Scene Two 6

Act Two **10**
   Scene One 10
   Scene Two 13
   Scene Three 18

Act Three **27**
   Scene One 27
   Scene Two 32

Act Four **36**
   Scene One 36
   Scene Two 40

Act Five **48**
   Scene One 48
   Scene Two 51

About the Author **59**

ACT ONE
SCENE ONE

Drummers, women, children, farmers, youths.

The palace of Itale in Ibaji kingdom. People of the land throughout. Women are busy cooking, and some are singing and dancing. The atmosphere is that of uncertainty; the old form of doing things, the passing of a great king, and the expectations of the people. From a distance, one can see what is happening as the Odafes, Gagos and the Okpalas are seated on stools by the right and the community elders by the left. The palace is wide enough to contain more than thirty people. The new king, Akalor, sits in the castle in the palace, ready to be crowned. The beads and the crown are by the right hand, and at the extreme end of the palace, drinks of many kinds are seen in their cartons. The upper section of the stage wall is covered with purple curtains, which are designed with different traditional artifacts. The priest holding the staff stares at any visitors as an invitation for a worship. The warriors are more appealing to behold; they represent all the generations and the ones yet to come.

NARRATOR

The rain will always fall, the season will always change, and when the rains fall, the shrubs and plants boost with the pride of new hope and beginning. Once there was darkness in our land. We hide our faces in shame and wander like sheep without a shepherd. I can see the sun rising and shining; it smiles with us like a new bride who has professed her wedding vows and is confident of the home she has chosen. But will she smile for long? The content of a nut is not known until it is cracked.

The Odafes, the Gagos, and the Okpalas enter in their regalia, all holding firm to their sticks and caps.

ODAFE

Let the trumpet sound, let the children play, let the women sing. For today is a memorable day; may we be blessed by the gods.

CHORUS

May we all sing and dance for joy.

ODAFE

May the pregnant day give birth to blessings, joy, peace, and love to our land.

CHORUS
May we all live long and prosper; may we all live to see our great grandchildren.

ODAFE
May our ancestors be pleased with our doings and open to us a great and wide heaven of providence and acceptance of their children. May today define our existence and be remembered for its uniqueness as we begin the harvest from our new trees.

CHORUS
Every child needs a father to protect him from danger and hurt, from rats and monkeys. We need a king to lead us. A good house without a roof is not a house.

GAGO
As the keeper of the tradition, I present to you a man who cheated death in his childhood. A man who was preserved by the gods and guarded by our ancestors. The son of Abgata the Great, who was the merchant of handsomeness and wisdom. A man with grandeur and charisma. The envy of every woman and the salt that has purified our land. The man who has served God and humanity, who has

traveled far and wide. A guardian of his people and fountain to all, James Onwuadiamu Akalor.

OKPALA

Praise is cheap; tears are cheaper when a good man is found. Today is pregnant, our expectations are high.

ODAFE

The content of a nut is not known until it is broken. Today...

He holds beads in his hand, while the other beads are lying on a stool. He uses these beads, formed into a crown, to crown the new king. He picks up one of each and thanks the gods before putting them on the right parts of the king's body; neck, wrist, and the waist.

ODAFE

This crown is the oldest among our people. It was forged by Enemaku the Great, who thought he could make himself king, but our ancestors said no, because the body must depend on the legs to move. You do not enter your grave by yourself, even if you dig it before you die. The crown refused to sit on his head until another man was chosen. We have mentioned names and we have enthroned kings but today sun comes out buzzing with life. This has shown that our ancestors are in consonance with our choice. As I put this crown on you, let the Lion curb and the lamb walk together. Let the wise and the foolish find counsel in you, the weak and the strong share your fortress. May the widows and the orphans rejoice in your providence and may you be the fountain of joy, comfort and protection to the old and the unborn.

TOWNSPEOPLE
So shall it be.

Women start singing and dancing. The cooks are busy with the pot. The men sit in the king's palace, while the younger men serve palm wine and other drinks.

Scene Two

The Itale community is busy with activities. The Odogwu are proceeding toward the new crowned king, leaves in their mouths, and their bodies marked with red and black camwood ashes. They have tied their heads with red cloths. The chief Odogwu leads the procession, shouting and chanting, as they scratch their cutlasses on the ground. The next group to follow is the Initiates. As they enter the palace, everyone expects trouble. The elders stand up in despair, but King Akalor remains calm as he addresses them.

KING AKALOR
The people of our land, the keepers and preservers of our culture and tradition, the warriors and defenders of our land: I welcome you to my palace. This is our land, the best place our parents left for us. A king is only a king when he has people around him. It is good that you are here and my elders are present. We shall listen to you, and we will work together to achieve our desires. Let me give you the opportunity to speak.

IFAH

The greatest Iroko that ever existed, our new and humble king: your wisdom is spoken of everywhere. I did not believe till now. Your words sparkle like fresh palm wine. I greet you. Our Odafes, Gagos, and Okpalas, whom the gods bestow with wisdom and foresight to protect and guide the king. Our elders, I greet you.

CHORUS

We greet you, too.

IFAH

We have come to welcome and congratulate you on your ascension to the throne of our ancestors.

KING AKALOR

Thank you for coming to us. I am encouraged by your visit, and pray that our people will smile once again.

IFAH

Communion with the gods is the highest fraternity bestowed with protection of the people and sustenance of our culture. On behalf of the fraternity, I wish you a peaceful and prosperous reign.

KING AKALOR
Thank you.

IFAH
Your Highness, I believe that the elders have intimated what is expected of you when we arrive.

KING AKALOR
We've had no opportunity to discuss that. However, since you are here, can you tell us yourself?

IFAH
If you must know, our conditions are non-negotiable. You seek our consent before making any decision, and whatever we do or say becomes a decree.

KING AKALOR
Is that all? I have heard you, but there is no need of seeking anyone's consent before replying you. I am a Christian who cannot partake in what you do and want. I have heard of your diabolical activities, which I know are not in line with our traditions. These are all alien to our Kingdom. The ancestors cannot enslave its own people.

IfAH

Your Highness, before you were many kings. Every Initiate has its demands. If you cannot give in to our demands, your reign will be inconsequential.

KING AKALOR

I have the staff of might that gives me power over everyone and everything in this community. If you have been feasting on other kings, then I warn you to quit your dubious business and follow the path of our ancestors. In fact, elders of our land, from today henceforth, by the powers bestowed on me, I ban all the activities of the Initiate. And so it shall be.

The king picks up his staff and goes to his bedchamber. The members of the Initiate stand speechless.

Act Two
Scene One

At the southern part of the village, not too far from a stream, is a large portion of plantation where Mama Ekele, a widow, maintains an orchard. She has been harvesting and selling from it for her children's upkeep. The plantation is at the nape of the village, where footpaths meet leading to Obiyo and Alu-Aja village.

Mama Ekele is seen weeding and stalking some plants in her plantation with her little baby wrapped on her back.

This baby is the child her husband died and left her three months pregnant with. Ifah had accused her of infidelity to his late brother just to oust her from her husband's land, which he wants to usurp. As she sees him, she braces up for any of his attacks.

IFAH
You stubborn woman, why do you dare to challenge me this much? A stubborn child

who dares his elders' instructions destroys his life.

MAMA EKELE

Good morning, sir! I hope you come in peace.

IFAH

May you never know peace again in your life if you mention peace again. What an insult!

MAMA EKELE

Sir, I didn't do anything wrong to you this morning; why are you insulting me this way? It is too early for this.

IFAH

What are you doing here this early morning? Have I not warned you to never come here again? Were you deaf when I boldly said so?

MAMA EKELE

Sir, I have shown you respect all my days in my husband's house before he died. Since he died, you have not given me peace. You took his car, took over his shop, and now you want to take this plantation from me. The plantation my husband and I laboured together to tend. You must be joking; I will not leave on your behalf.

IFAH
The next time I see you on this land, I will chop off your hands before removing your head from its neck.

MAMA EKELE
I have heard you say this even to my late husband. I will not hesitate to report you to the kinsmen. You said these words, and my husband is gone, six feet under, just as you warned him. I will report you to the elders of the family.

She picks up her basket and water jar. She also picks up the cutlass and other things she brought from home and lifts it all to her head. She starts heading back home, fuming with anger.

IFAH
Never come back, useless woman! I will send you to your husband the next time I see you here. Marry me you refused and you want to take and enjoy my brother's property, I am also his property. God has saved you, you would have visited the morgue by now. Report me to the president not the elders. I am not even scared of them.

He exits.

Scene Two

At the marketplace, a woman sits very close to some young men selling rice, yam and fish. She is carried away by what the boys are discussing. The market has been recently renovated, and some new buildings and stalls can be seen. The market also leads to king's palace. Mama Ekele stands behind the woman for a long period of time, but the woman is too absentminded to notice that someone is behind her. You can hear songs and chants of different kinds, depending on what the person is selling. Choruses instruct the shoppers to "buy rice," "buy yams," and "buy fish," etc.

MAMA EKELE
(to the market woman)
My friend ,what bothers you this much, that I and my shadow cannot be seen?

EJURA
My sister, I am so sorry. I was busy hearing what our youths are saying about our community.

MAMA EKELE
Anything good coming out of them?

EJURA
Who would have believed that our youth could be this organized and empowered?

MAMA EKELE
How? What happened to them?

EJURA
You see these boys? Many of them were thieves, some were used as thugs to cause problems, and many other atrocities. Now look at them, glowing with life.

MAMA EKELE
This shows that our king has kept to his promise of making everyone in the community responsible.

EJURA
Hmmm, look at our market, it has attracted many people and many buyers who come from far and near. Look at how the market flows with people. It doesn't sting like before. We make good sales and make profits from what we sell.

MAMA EKELE

How did these people here get access to the goods sold here?

EJURA

Our king brought people from outside our community the day this hospital was launched. See them! From criminals to tycoons.

MAMA EKELE

I want to affirm to you that our land will progress with this our king. He is a god, sent to help liberate us from the shackle of wicked men in this community.

EJURA

We pray that our ancestors will protect him from the wicked ones.

MAMA EKELE

My sister, before I forget why I am here. You know my husband's younger brother?

EJURA

Ifah, that devil born? What has he done this time around?

MAMA EKELE
He met me in my late husband's plantation and threatened to behead me the next time he sees me there.

EJURA
I have told you to report him since your husband was alive. Now he has succeeded in killing your husband. Is your turn to be fed to the earth.

MAMA EKELE
I reported him to his kinsmen when he said he would kill my husband, but they did nothing about it.

EJURA
What! So everybody in your husband's clan is scared of him?

MAMA EKELE
Yes, it looks like he has become a lion of the family. Nobody wants to confront him, because they don't want to die.

EJURA
Then take it to the king, because this man will either kill you or make you leave everything for him to inherit.

MAMA EKELE

Will the king listen to me? Won't he be scared of him? He has been a nightmare to everybody. All he does is to eliminate anyone who dares to challenge him.

EJURA

My sister, try the king for once, because when all the cocks are killed, of what value is the hen? Who will crow to wake us at daybreak?

MAMA EKELE

I am too scared to report him to the king. Suppose I get laughed at if the king, too, can do nothing?

EJURA

You either do something or die in silence.

MAMA EKELE

Ok, I will give it a trial. Let me go and cook for my baby. I will let you know if anything comes up. Take care of yourself and your family.

EJURA

Please be careful, and take care of yourself.

Scene Three

The king's palace. It is a large room with colourful paintings and designs. The artist took his time in molding the two lions by the left and right hand sides of the higher part of the house, which looks like a pulpit. The palace looks clean and well-furnished, with two different colours of seats designed that can accommodate 14-16 people. The king and two sets of elders known by the colours of their cloaks are seen sitting, facing each other. The king sits on his throne, well-dressed in his royal regalia, and two guards stand on each side with stern faces.

KING AKALOR
I welcome you all to this great and blessed moment. It is my honour, and a rare privilege, to have the elders from two great kingdom come together and sit down to discuss the issues that have been breaking us apart. I greet the great warriors and elders from the Akuro kingdom, where my mother comes from. I know not whether, because of the maternal bond between us, it will be difficult for you to come. Before greener pastures called us to

different homes, you were here. It is your home; please feel relaxed to deliberate on what we are going to discuss. Once more, welcome.

ATAGWUBA

My lord, we appreciate you for every painful step you have taken to set our community on track. We thank you so much. I find it hard to accept the particular gesture that brought us here this early morning. Why do you invite these dog eaters here? You know that we do not dine with them nor sit in a gathering with them, and we have not since they decided to kill our women in their farmland. My fellow elders, have I spoken your minds?

ELDERS OF ITALE

Yes, you have spoken our minds.

KING AKALOR

Elders of our great land, what is greatness without wisdom? I plead with you to give me audience and have patience for the sake of these elders, who put aside their grievances to hear and listen to us.

ELDERS OF THE AKURO KINGDOM

King of the Itale kingdom, we greet you. Elders of this kingdom, we bring you greetings from our great king. They say when the sky is heavy with rain, it makes a heavy downpour. Our son, your king, has given us reason to sheath our swords and seek peace. If our coming here is a problem, we shall seek our leave.

KING AKALOR

Our elders, no matter how heavy the rainfall, it cannot wash the leopard skin. What have we benefited from all our wars, rancour, slanders, and disunity?

ELDERS OF THE AKURO KINGDOM

When God wants to bless a land, he gives them a son full of wisdom as their king. You have a king that the gods have endowed with great wisdom. The ants must come and learn from him. We beg you again to give him listening ears.

ATAGWUBA

My fellow elders, how will the head beg the legs and the legs deny him? We have heard him, and he wants us to listen to him, should we not allow this meeting to take place?

The elders look at each other and nod their heads.

ATAGWUBA

Ok, we can begin, your highness. The elders have given you their approval.

KING AKALOR

My elders, you all have proven to me that you have great concern for our land. Posterity will judge you, and your names will all be written in gold. We have been fighting for years without any break. We have stopped every development that should have come to our lands, because we fight and scare people from coming to our land to give us good things. What have we benefitted from the blood we shed and our brothers whose lives we have cut short?

The elders start muttering, blaming each other for what the king has said. He clears his throat and continues.

KING AKALOR

I called us here after I had discussed with my brother, the king of Akuro, the peace we need, and the ways we can unite ourselves and bring development to our lands. We want your people to come here freely, and we want our people go to your land and come back unharmed.

ATAGWUBA

Your Highness, it is hard to believe this hope will ever come to fruition. It can only be achieved if these people here accept the fact that they are subordinate to us. We were created before them. Our ancestors were here before them, but they want us to share everything with them. They must respect us.

ELDERS OF THE AKURO KINGDOM

You see, when God created your ancestors, the first thing he gave them was a plate of pride. We came here knowing full well that you would be stubborn, even toward your son the king. What is the use of a cap if it cannot cover the head?

ELDERS OF ITALE

The roots of a tree do not look for infertile land, because it will either be stunted or die. No matter what grudges we bear against each other, we must put them aside and seek what will benefit us as a people. We are first humans before we are descendants, and we have the same ancestor, since we speak the same language and share the same culture. If I have your support, let us continue to discuss progress rather than backwardness.

All in chorus answer affirmatively.

KING AKALOR
I thank you all for this peaceful resolution. However, before we continue, here is a keg of palm wine and some kola nuts. We must follow our ancestors' steps. Let us break kola nuts and eat some bush meat before we lay our hands on the staff of peace, to seal our covenants and friendship.

King Akalor takes kola nut and prays to the gods. He breaks the nut as the elders all respond and pick up one each. They eat and drink to their satisfaction. The king clears his throat and starts the discussion.

KING AKALOR
I have traveled to many places and have many friends. Some of these friends have promised to come and develop our land for us. Based on those promises, we are starting with the construction of a road that links our communities so that businesses can boom. The company I worked with in Kaduna is coming to open a textile company here in our land,

and I want it to be on the land we have been fighting on so that we will benefit from it peacefully.

ELDERS OF THE AKURO KINGDOM

If putting that land to use will stop this fighting, we are willing to let it go, and we wish that whatever proceeds are made from it, we shall share it. All we want is an assurance from the king.

KING AKALOR

Our people say, he who has bad intentions towards his brothers cannot eat from the same plate with him. As a step towards our brotherliness, we shall have equal responsibilities and allocation in the market, and we shall sit together to share and discuss the affairs of the market.

They all agree and are about to leave when a woman comes in, shouting and calling for help. They all decide to sit down again and wait to listen to her.

KING AKALOR

Woman, what is it? Why are you disturbing the peace of the kingdom?

MAMA EKELE

My king and my elders, I greet you. What is the frog's joy of being in water when the water is boiling? The vulture would not have a bald head if nature did not cheat it. Your highness, my house is burning just because I have no roof to protect me.

KING AKALOR

Who is after your life? Speak without fear.

MAMA EKELE

My husband's younger brother is throwing stones at me and wants to kill me if I don't leave his brother's house.

KING AKALOR

In this land, who is your husband?

MAMA EKELE

Late Ejembi of Akunala kindred. The one that died on his farmland.

KING AKALOR

I see. Who is this his brother?

MAMA EKELE

Ifah, the troublemaker who was behind the death of my husband. He took all my husband's belongings after he was buried and still threatens me with death if I do not leave the only land he left behind.

KING AKALOR

The troublemaker? Guards, go and bring him here and now. It is time that we should know that women are also human beings. They must be given the opportunities to do more in the society. They must be listened to and treated well.

ACT THREE
SCENE ONE

Ifah is lamenting as he returns from the king's palace. He looks like a baby chick who has been beaten by heavy rain. He speaks to himself as he walks through the thick, bushy road that leads to the village square. Behind the village square are groups of buildings that the king has built through the support of the World Bank. He has named the area SOCIAL CENTRE, a place where recreational activities take place. There are bars, motels, canteens, and a lot more.

IFAH
From where does he think he comes? Did he not leave this village in his childhood to avoid being killed by the gods? Now he becomes king and he thinks he is fearless. I will deal with him. He thinks because of what he is doing to us that I will leave him. Let me stop by here and help myself to some bottles. I don't want to see this useless woman again in my entire life.

As he continues entering, he meets his friends Ojoneh and Ikoijo. These three are known universally as longtime friends who have never argued. They visit each other for pleausre, not only when they are in trouble.

OJONEH

The greatest god of our time and our land. The no-go area and the only king of his kingdom. It is good that you have come.

IFAH

My friends and the only lions of our kingdom. You did not tell me you would be here this hot afternoon.

IKOIJO

Since business is no longer flourishing in our land, this is the only place that calms our nerves.

OJONEH

You looked troubled, my friend. Has business failed you as well?

IFAH

My brothers, did you know that I have never thought a day like this would come? What do you say if the king of the jungle is threatened?

IKOIJO
My friend, it means you don't have a kingdom and you need to do something.

OJONEH
I hope that witch has not reported you to the king.

IFAH
I have never known that a man born of a woman could threaten me. Do you know, he not only warned me; he said that if anything happens to her - whether hunger, illness or death - I will be castrated. He told me this! A human being telling me this nonsense.

Ifah's two friends laugh as if they might burst.

IFAH
Hmmm! I have been relegated to a nobody and a laughingstock.

OJONEH
If I know my friend will sit and hear this from a man, and the man still lives, I will not agree. So what did you tell him?

IKOIJO
And did you not bring his head to the table?

IFAH

Do you know, all the elders and some strange looking elders from Itale shut me up. The king says if it is trouble I want, I should say it openly so that they can take action.

IKOIJO

So this man meant what he said on his coronation. He has been encouraged because he is chosen by the gods.

OJONEH

Do you know that people don't run away whenever they see us anymore? We have lost our powers because of this man. Even the boys we send do not want to do business with us. Because he calls and warns them.

IFAH

We are losing our grip and running out of money. My brother's wife openly celebrated my downfall today. She will soon come for her husband's car and business.

IKOIJO

What do we do now? This is worse than death itself. My neighbor saw me today and started laughing. We must do something or leave this community before we get paraded around as fools.

IFAH

Me, I will not give up. I will go to our source and gather more strength. I will come back and claim what belongs to me. Whatever I say must be accepted by everyone, including the king.

OJONEH

That is the only solution; we must deal with these people. They must know that where lions exist, the gazelles shouldn't use the land as their play field.

IFAH

My friends, let us drink to our sorrows and plan for a takeover.

SCENE TWO

The palace of the king. It is as beautiful as always. Guards and maidens are seen running errands as usual. The palace is a multiple-story building, with each of the princes and princesses having their own rooms. A very large garden with space that can host people numbering in the thousands sits by the right entrance of the gate. People gather, and different dance groups are seen performing. Dignitaries and elders are seen sitting in groups of four at decorated tables with assorted bottled drinks and palm wine served in wooden cups. The king sits by a man in a black suit with a clean-shaven beard. He looks either American or British.

>MASTER OF CEREMONY
>Thank you for a wonderful performance. I know that the whole world knows that we have great culture and traditions. Our dance is among the best, and that is the reason our visitors are carried away by its frenzy. May I have the singular privilege to welcome the Iroko of our land, the greatest god of our people and the convener of peace. The only

voice that gives hope to the hopeless and carrier of good justice. The Solomon of our time, full of wisdom and blessed by the gods themselves. The only king that evil respects. Ladies and gentlemen, His Royal Highness Chief James Onwuadiamu Akalor the Onu-Itale!

The people shout and clap joyfully, welcoming the king as he stands up. A gun is fired to the sky, and drums and the ogene follow a rapturous cheer.

KING AKALOR

Ladies and Gentlemen, all the Gagos, the Odafes and Okpalas from the two kingdoms, my brother the king of Akuro. I thank you for being part of this great and historic moment. Today marks a very crucial and most valuable day in the history of our lands. This ceremony is supposed to be held in the market square, but because of its value, we the two kings agreed that it should happen here, in my palace. There is no king without subjects. We must embrace and appreciate each other. We are not just celebrating our unity, but also signing an agreement to construct the road which starts from Akuro to Ikaka. It will help in our trade with other communities. It will bring in many things that we do not know. I would like to welcome a foreigner in our midst, for he has brought good things to us. We have decided to give them a portion of land to build their business and to help construct the roads. Let me welcome him officially to speak to us. My brother will speak when we finish. Mr. Malcolm, you are most welcome, and can you speak to our people so that we know your intentions better?

MR. MALCOLM

Let me greet the two kings, who have sheathed their swords to pave ways for development and quit their former bloodbath. Congratulations to all of us, because we leave as people to be responsible for anything we do. I have come to represent my country in looking at the proposed work we have agreed to do here. Your king has been our good friend for a long time. We asked him what he wants us to do for him. The King wants us to develop his community instead of building mansions for him. He is a good man with a kind heart. The type of people that are true leaders are rare. You need to thank God for him and thank him for his good heart. This project is one among many that we shall bring to you. We are coming to invest in tourism and agriculture. We shall bring good, improved species of crops for better use. I sign this contract today for the better use of your people, and for all humanity.

Malcolm removes the pen from his pocket and signs the document of agreement. The people shout for joy and chant "Thank you! Thank you!! Thank you!!!"

As the day progresses, the people dance and make merry as the sound of drums fade out.

Act Four
Scene One

Four years have passed, and the people have experienced peace all this while. The community has changed: modern buildings and artifacts are seen everywhere. Business in the community has expanded to building of factories. Farmers have companies coming to buy their farms' produce, to take everything they can get and then manufacture. Schools of different levels have been built. The community that once was a mundane village of local people has now become the center of commerce and socialization. Everybody around lives peacefully, and you can notice smiles on their faces.

In the heat of a discussion, some women are seen busy selling and throwing banter at each other. In Unane's shop. Four women: Unane, Anechido, Afor, and Enefola sit on a mat and discuss and share ideas.

AFOR
I would have never imagined that by this time,
I would have a business that is mine.

ENEFOLA
I thought it was not possible when I saw the foundation of this plaza. I thought this calm would never come. Everybody drinks and goes home at any time, not like the last ten years, when people would run even at day time because of some criminal-minded people and the Odogus.

UNANE
I remember when my father died, the traditionalists came and demanded that my elder brother be initiated before my father could even be buried.

ANECHIDO
These people have spoilt our culture with their greed and diabolic means of extortion.

UNANE
Just imagine the number of people that died at their hands. Good people that God had blessed with thought, who would have developed this community more if they were alive.

AFOR
If these men were alive, the king would have gotten more support for his good works.

ENEFOLA
Just imagine what our faith would be if it were Ifah that was made the king.

UNANE
Ewo! We would have all died... or relocated to a far, unknown land.

ANECHIDO
He fought for this throne and frustrated many people who contested with him.

AFOR
This man is a devil. If not for the strength of the gods, our king would have been dead by now.

UNANE
A man who killed his brother because of jealousy and land. He also threatened to kill the poor widow, and would have, if not for the resilience of the king.

ENEFOLA
I wonder if he even fears the king.

As the women are talking, Ifah passes by.

ANECHIDO

Speak of the devil - here he comes.

UNANE

Did he hear us?

AFOR

Do you still fear him?

UNANE

I just don't want to die young.

AFOR

He will not do anything to anyone. A toothless bulldog is fiercer than him.

They all laugh.

Exit.

Scene Two

In a beer parlor. The place is divided into four parts. The VIP corner is decorated with red linen. Each table has four chairs, with a vase of flowers in the middle. The bulb in that section shines dimly. This space is overtly meant for the rich, and for people who are real customers who come to rest with women of easy virtue - for a price. The cost of their own drinks and pepper soup is double the price of those who are in the common bar. The exotic bar is for those who sell or buy secret goods. Men who secretly sleep with their neighbours' wives and daughters, drug dealers, assassins and other criminals sit there. The last section is for everybody. The village gluttons sit there and drink. Their own prices are less, and in most cases, when the first two parts are full, they are served last. They may even shout four or more times before being served. Ifah sits in the exotic bar at the extreme end, waiting impatiently for whoever he is waiting for. After a while, four Odogwus and six fierce-looking boys join him. They bow and sit down. Everyone begins to drink copious amounts of whiskey.

ODOGWU 1

The greatest god of our land, the fiercest and dreaded Lion of the jungle. I greet you.

IFAH

It is only a stupid child that thinks he can challenge his mother while knowing that he depends on her for breast milk.

ODOGWU 2

The only moment that gives me joy is dealing with those bastards.

ODOGWU 1

We hope that this call will trigger us to get back to who we were. I have been spit on severely, and mocked by people who once feared me. I have been made a subject of ridicule and laughter. My heart is on fire right now, primed for destruction. I hope that I have spoken the minds of the remaining Odogwus.

The Odogwus answer affirmatively in a chorus.

IFAH

Ok, cruel men of the night, I owe you much, and this we must do to reclaim our might and fame. This night, I shall gather all my friends, and you must not fail to meet us at the valley of castration. I warn again, this plan must be sealed in your head, and you must not eat a woman's food before coming.

ODOGWU 1
Thank you very much, our captain and the greatest god.

Everyone polishes off their whiskey, and then exits.

In the night, darkness is everywhere. People have retired to their houses, except for those who keep late nights at the bar, watering their unquenched taste for beer and loose women. The three men always referred to as demons, Ifah, Ojoneh, and Ikoijo, sit under a tree covered with thick shrubs, all in red clothes. The Odogwus clear their throats and enter the enclave. They sit in a circle, as if being remote-controlled by the spirits. The three friends sit on the three stones facing each other, ready for business. Ifah stands up with a calabash and a knife. The trio holds their hands together and chants some common incantations with their eyes fixed on a pot in center of them. Then, the chief Odogwu brings a white rooster and slaughters it, pouring the stain on their hand. They sit down, break kola, and start discussing.

IFAH

My brothers, we are gathered here today to renew our bond and oath to our mighty Ogenega. We all know what it takes and what we used to be. We beg for strength and power, that we shall be able to control the community as it was before we were ruined. Once again, the bond of our fraternity and great brotherhood is back with great force and desire for destruction.

OJONEH

I wish to warn us that we must be firm in whatever we do. Hit without mercy, and be brutal.

IKOIJO

We were in charge of everything in this community,. We decided who becomes king and what he must do. But now, we are stripped of our power.

OJONEH

The chicken who lost its beak to the fire must always use its claws to destroy fire wherever it sees it.

IFAH

We were caught unaware and had no clue that the Odafes would betray us. I asked the two of you to be closer to the kingmakers so that I could become the king, but you failed, certainly because you thought I was doing this just for myself.

IKOIJO

We must discuss what to do to redeem our faces from the people if we want to gain back our respect. What do we do now?

OJONEH

Let's draw our swords against the king.

IFAH

No, the people will stone us to death. We shall go to his palace and spell out our demands. If he refuses, we shall throw the might of Ogenega upon him to kill him gradually.

ODOGWU 1

What if he refuses to die? Just have your boys finish him. We will creep into his bedchamber and kill him quietly.

IFAH

No, we shall do the usual tomorrow morning. We shall go to his palace, and he must listen to us. If he doesn't do what we want, we will do the needful.

They drink a concoction in a calabash, and then exit.

The next morning, people start running. The Odogwus are in front, led by their leader and Ojoneh, Ikoijo, and Ifah following behind. Everybody is afraid, because they have not seen them out for over ten years. As they enter the palace, everybody knows there is a problem. The king is in his palace sitting on his throne and having a meeting with his elders. Everybody is startled when they enter uninvited.

>KING AKALOR
>What childish attitude is this? Who gave you the impetus to enter my palace without excuse?

>IFAH
>We have come to ask for what was rightfully ours from you, our king.

>OJONEH
>Oh yes, these chiefs know the truth. They should tell you the normal way things are done in this community.

>KING AKALOR
>I know who you are. And I know how things worked in this village before I was enthroned as king.

IFAH

We need you to support us and give us what other kings gave us. You must give to Caesar what belongs to him. He who collects the leprous man's property must be ready to shave him.

KING AKALOR

My brothers, things have changed. I did not take anything from anyone, so please stop disturbing the peace of this community. I am the son of this community, and an equal heir to this throne. Leprosy aside, we should know that we cannot accept evil in place of good. Day has broken; there is no hiding place for evil. Modernity has come to change the bad ways in which things were done.

Ikoijo signals the Odogwu, and he drops a rotten egg. The elders run away, except for the king and his body guards.

KING AKALOR

I am the Moses of my time. I don't fear you or your diabolic plans. I am covered by the shadow of God the Most High. Whatever you do will not affect me, except as God wills it.

His guards want to fight them, but the king stops them.

> KING AKALOR
> Allow them to go.

They exit.

ACT FIVE
SCENE ONE

Three weeks after the visit of Ifah and his friends, the king has been hospitalized. The people keep praying for the king, but there are no changes. The chiefs gather to plead with him to give in to Ifah's request, but he can't. At the palace the next day, he dies.

Singing and drumming in pain and mourning as King Akalor dies. Enter Queen Patricia, wife of Akalor. She dresses in white linen as she mourns her husband. She is accompanied by elderly women in procession to her room. Next, Ajuma and siblings mourn the departure of The Great King.

NARRATOR
It is a painful one, indeed. Life is brief.

AJUMA
It's more painful when it's unexpected.

Omoja enters. He is a culprit who sits and pretends, casting his strings and passing them off as objects of divination.

NARRATOR
Omoja, the eldest of all in this community, I greet you.

Mother mourns, children mourn.

Now, all mourn the untimely death of The Great King.

Omoja moves aside as Queen Patricia and the children prepare to lay King Akalor to rest.

Now Omoja tells wives and children of the pains that the death of the King has caused to the land of Itale Kingdom. He tells them the agony that befalls the community.

OMOJA
King Akalor is a great man, born to reign and rule, but death took him unawares.

The townspeople softly sing a dirge as the king's corpse is laid to rest.

The Narrator hums.

NARRATOR

Wife weeps, children weep. As they console one another in their pains. As King Akalor finally goes home. Townspeople sing and mourn as they disperse.

Scene Two

In the king's palace, the king is dead. Some sit on the floor, and some sit on benches in black clothes, wailing. The Gagos, Odafes, and Okpalas are seen in a serious discussion. The Odogwus are all in a sad and dangerous mood. The people of Itale arrange themselves solemnly about the stage. Light dims on Narrator; he moves into the sorrowful crowd of Townspeople as he consoles them in a soft tune.

NARRATOR
The events of our lives can only be reflected in a mirror. My tongue is heavy; I cannot speak. It is the ugly surface of a man's innermost thought that is spoken in dreams, or in a state of unconsciousness. I am a sojourner in this world and cannot be the prophet with bad news. Where are these boys? Adino, Okajale, and Oyaka, have you finished setting the stage? Let the people watch this and judge for themselves if our king has done great things. To be sure, he is a true hero.

ADINO
Yes, the stage is set, and I will act as the Odogwu.

OKAJALE
I want to be a very dangerous man and a troublemaker.

OYAKE
I want to be the king; I like his role.

NARRATOR
How do we get new characters?

OJOGBANE
I am here.

NARRATOR
In a land far beyond where we are, a king was born, he led his people, and he died. Our testimonies at the graveyard may not be enough to demonstrate what the King has done. But as these people from his land tell us more, we shall see him through them.

ADINO
My brothers, Oyaka the king is dead. How do we bury him?

OJOGBANE
He will be buried as other kings.

EGWUDA
King Akalor was the greatest king we ever had in our community. He deserves to be buried well, according to his choice.

ADINO
He brought a lot of modern things to develop our land. He has really shown us that humanity finds its strength in oneness. He trusted in the hand and might of God. He has never taken part in our ancient tradition of ritual cleansing and lineage sacrifice before becoming a king. His hands were clean, and his tongue has never tasted anything bad. He will be buried the way his family wants it.

OKAJALE
I am broken to my bones. The King has shown commitment and dedication, even till death. Like a lamb, he was sacrificed, and he did not complain or defend himself. Our desire to always get what we want and be feared the most turns us into beasts. But in this man, King Akalor, is found meekness and humanity. His life and sacrifices, his sacrifices from birth, have lit the path he took to glory.

Do we need another messiah to come? No, God knows why he made him escape death from childhood. When his father was killed and he was ousted 30 years ago, who would have thought he would return to take the throne of his forefather?

ADINO

We have tried to initiate him, but he stood his ground. He insisted on justice for all and feared no one till he died. He gave his body and soul to his community and found refuge in God. I admire him even in death. The queen has demanded that he be buried the Christian way. What do we do? Should we keep tradition away, or stand by our custom?

OKAJALE

We were born to be custodians of our culture and traditions. These are made by men like us to guide us, but in our most fearful, darkest hearts, we have tampered with these cultures and traditions to suit our desires. We brought in some dubiousness and cheated the people, forcefully confiscated what belongs to them, made them eat sand at their prime in the grave, and we still live to talk of tradition? Let this great king be buried in Christ, the way the family wants it.

ADINO
Tell the family that we have agreed that our king, Akalor the Great, will be given a befitting burial in the church so that he will continue to watch over us and intercede on our behalf in God's presence.

They exit.

In the village of Itale, the community has been in mourning. The people are anxiously waiting for the arrival of their late king's corpse for burial. The great St. John the Ascension Catholic Church is filled with people coming from different walks of life, and more than ten priests are already in the church waiting. All of a sudden, the community bursts with noise at the blaring of siren. The noise from the crowd is the mixture of dirges and the sounds of the Odogwus, who are dancing and chanting. Joining the cacophony are the sound of cars and motorcycles accompanying the ambulance. People run and follow the ambulance.

ADINO
What shall we say? Our eyes have seen and our ears have heard. This man was a great king, and I hope we will not regret losing him as our leader. Look at how the people mourn and weep for him. They follow him even to death.

OYAKA

If this man had lived a little longer, if he was not cut short by the wicked, we would grow bigger and better. Our village would turn to a city, and we would be a better people.

ADINO

Why do you say, "if he was not cut short"?

OYAKA

Are you a visitor in this community? He has helped the masses and has stood for them, so that freedom becomes their daily manner. He clipped the wings of the wicked and gave the weak wings to fly. He has made our community a heaven, where many become angels. His success made people like you jealous, and you began plotting his death.

ADINO

My brother, they say ignorance breeds doom, and if you are not careful, you will kill the goose that lays the golden egg. A pot does not know the value of water until it is burnt by fire. We were more enveloped by greed and selfishness than by the interest of the people.

IFAH

I have been quiet for all this time, not because I don't have the words to say, but because I was so foolish as to allow the devil to use me to cause problems in my community, for my own people. How can I redeem myself after this? Will our ancestors ever forgive us? Will the living? Adino, I am sorry to have misled you, and I am sorry for all the problems I have caused. I shall meet all my friends and leave this community in shame. But our king was a hero and a pace-setter. I pray the people will forgive me, and I pray that the king will watch over his people even in death.

He goes out weeping, and the others follow him.

END OF PLAY.

ABOUT THE AUTHOR

THE AUTHOR Halima Onoja is one of the fast rising female writers from North Central, Nigeria. She holds B. A. English Language and Literature, Post-graduate Diploma in Education, and a Master of English Education from the University of Jos. Onoja is a member of several professional bodies, including the Literary Scholars Association of Nigeria (LSAN), English Scholars Association of Nigeria (ESAN) and Association of Nigerian Authors (ANA). She lectures at the Department of English, Federal University of Education, Pankshin, Plateau State. Her recent book, 'The Basics of Writing: Tips for Expressing Impressive Ideas in Print' is in the press.

www.ingramcontent.com/pod-product-compliance
Lightning Source LLC
Chambersburg PA
CBHW042130100526
44587CB00026B/4242